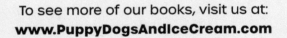

EARN

FACTS

SIZE

EIGHT

CATION

ES 3-10

# THE FANTASTIC WORLD OF

# Bugs

Danae Wolfe, Owner of
**Chasing Bugs
Conservation Education**

**FUN FACTS**
About Our
Tiny Friends

# About the Author and Photographer

What's your first thought when you see a bug? Perhaps the words **EW, ICKY, or GROSS** come to mind? Want to know what I think when I see a bug? **AWESOME! COOL! BEAUTIFUL**! Yep, I love bugs! And I think you should too!

Hello friends! My name is Danae and I think insects and spiders—also called bugs—are some of the most amazing animals in the world. From our large insects like giant silk moths to our cute spiders like jumping spiders, I think all bugs are great! But I haven't always loved bugs. In fact, when I was a kid, I really disliked insects and spiders. It's true! I spent much of my childhood running away from anything with six or eight legs. Bugs seemed so creepy to me. Thankfully, **that all changed when I got my first camera**. As a teenager, I began taking photos of insects and spiders and, from behind the lens, I began to look at bugs in a whole new way. Today, I love introducing people of all ages to the beauty and diversity of our buggy world.

From the soils to the seas to the skies, bugs are everywhere around us and **they have important roles to play in the world**. Insects and spiders pollinate our flowers, help decompose fallen trees and dead animals, and balance food webs by eating - or being eaten by - other animals. It might be hard to believe, but without bugs, the world would look a lot different.

Join me in exploring the fantastic world of bugs. The pages of this book will introduce you to some of the **insects and spiders you might find in your own backyard**. After reading about our many-legged friends, I encourage you to head outside and start exploring! Look under rocks, roll over logs, or take a stroll through the garden and you're sure to make friends with a few fascinating bugs. Happy bug-hunting!

**Danae Wolfe**
Owner of Chasing Bugs Conservation Education

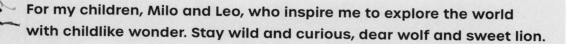

For my children, Milo and Leo, who inspire me to explore the world with childlike wonder. Stay wild and curious, dear wolf and sweet lion.

# Giant Silk Moth

*Saturniidae*

**Pictured is a Luna Moth (*Actias luna*)**

# FUN FACTS

Adult giant silk moths do not have mouths and do not eat. Living for just a week or two, the primary role of adult moths is reproduction. Adult giant silk moths are among the most colorful moths.

Males have long, feathery antennae

Their larvae form are able to spin threads of silk which we use for making fabric

Their bodies are covered in thick hair

Their colorful patterns help with camouflage for defense against predators

### Where do they live?
Every continent except Antarctica

### How big are they?
Wingspans of 4-6 inches = a dollar bill

### What do they eat?
Caterpillars (larvae) feed on plants. Adults do not feed.

# Honey Bee

## *Apidae*

**Pictured is a Western Honey Bee (*Apis mellifera*)**

# FUN FACTS

There are over 20,000 species of bees in the world, but only 8 species are honey bees. *Apis mellifera*, or the western honey bee, is native to Eurasia, but has been domesticated in North America and used as a pollinator for some crops including blueberries and almonds.

They use their great sense of smell to find flowers and communicate in the hive

Bees can flap their wings up to 200 times per second

Pollen baskets on their hind legs are where they store pollen to bring back to their nest

Their hairy bodies aid in pollinating the flowers they visit

**Where do they live?**
Every continent except Antarctica

**How big are they?**
Up to 3/4 inch = a dime

**What do they eat?**
Nectar and pollen

# Ant

*Formicidae*

**Pictured is a Wood Ant (*Formica* species)**

# FUN FACTS

Ant colonies range in size from a few dozen individuals to millions of ants living in highly organized colonies. The largest known ant colony in the world is located in Southern Europe and spans more than 3,700 miles.

Some species of ant queens can live for up to 30 years

Ants can be red or black in color and some even have stripes

Their strong bodies can lift up to 20 times their own weight

Two strong jaws (called mandibles) are used to carry food or construct its nests

## Where do they live?
Every continent except Antarctica

## How big are they?
Up to 1.5 inches =
a Lego mini-figure

## What do they eat?
Insects, plants, and nectar

# Praying Mantis

*Mantodea*

**Pictured is a Chinese Praying Mantis (*Tenodera sinensis*)**

# FUN FACTS

Praying mantises are great hunters thanks to their ability to see in 3D through stereo vision, and their ability to swivel their head 360 degrees. While mantises feed largely on insects and spiders, they have been known to eat frogs, snakes, and even hummingbirds.

aying mantises
ve a total of 5
es, 2 large eyes
the side of
eir heads and
much smaller
es in the middle

They come in a wide variety of colors to blend in with flowers

They stay completely still and camouflaged before striking their prey

Their forelegs are pincers which they use to catch prey

## Where do they live?
Every continent except Antarctica

## How big are they?
Up to 6 inches = a dollar bill

## What do they eat?
Insects and spiders

# Leafhopper

*Cicadellidae*

**Pictured is a Candy-Striped Leafhopper (*Graphocephala coccinea*)**

# FUN FACTS

Despite their small size, leafhoppers can jump up to 100 times the length of their body, thanks to their specialized hind legs. As you walk through the garden, you can see leafhoppers hopping from one plant to another.

Their short antennae below the eyes resemble cat whiskers

A leafhopper can jump in any direction, even backwards, thanks to their special hind legs

They have piercing, sucking mouth parts that they use to feed on plant sap

They range in color from browns and grays to shades of blue, red, yellow, and green

## Where do they live?
Every continent except Antarctica

## How big are they?
Up to 1/2 inch = a marble

## What do they eat?
Plant sap

# Lady Beetle

## *Coccinellidae*

**Pictured is a Multi-Colored Asian Lady Beetle (*Harmonia axyridis*)**

# FUN FACTS

Lady beetles are often used to control pests like aphids in the garden. While they have large appetites for other insects, these beetles have a good defense to avoid being eaten by other animals. Their brightly colored bodies send a warning that they do not taste good!

When the weather gets too cold, lady beetles hibernate

While many lady beetles are red or pink with black spots, others are yellow, orange, or even black and some are spotless

They breathe through small openings on the abdomen and thorax called spiracles

Their large wings fold up underneath the exterior shell for protection

**Where do they live?**
Every continent except Antarctica

**How big are they?**
Up to 3/4 inch = a dice

**What do they eat?**
Aphids and soft-bodied insects

# Blow Fly

### *Calliphoridae*

**Pictured is a Common Green Bottle Fly (*Lucilia sericata*)**

# FUN FACTS

Larval blow flies feed on dead and decaying animal tissues, making them great decomposers and an important part of ecosystems. You might find blow flies lingering around the trash can or dog waste.

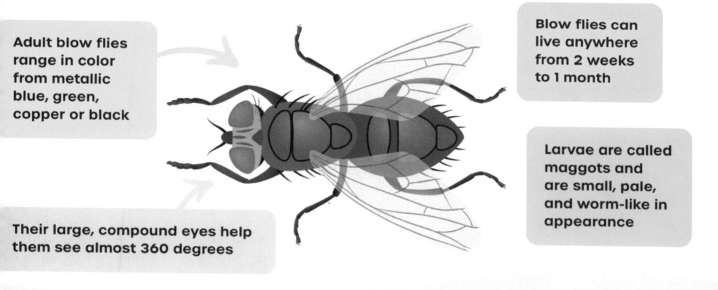

Adult blow flies range in color from metallic blue, green, copper or black

Blow flies can live anywhere from 2 weeks to 1 month

Larvae are called maggots and are small, pale, and worm-like in appearance

Their large, compound eyes help them see almost 360 degrees

## Where do they live?
Every continent except Antarctica

## How big are they?
Up to 1/2 inch = a push pin

## What do they eat?
Animal waste, animal tissue, nectar, and pollen

# Skimmer Dragonfly

*Libellulidae*

**Pictured is a Meadowhawk Dragonfly (*Sympetrum* species)**

# FUN FACTS

Dragonflies are among the greatest predators in the world. Scientists have found that dragonflies have up to a 95% success rate in capturing prey, compared to about a 25% success rate of a lion.

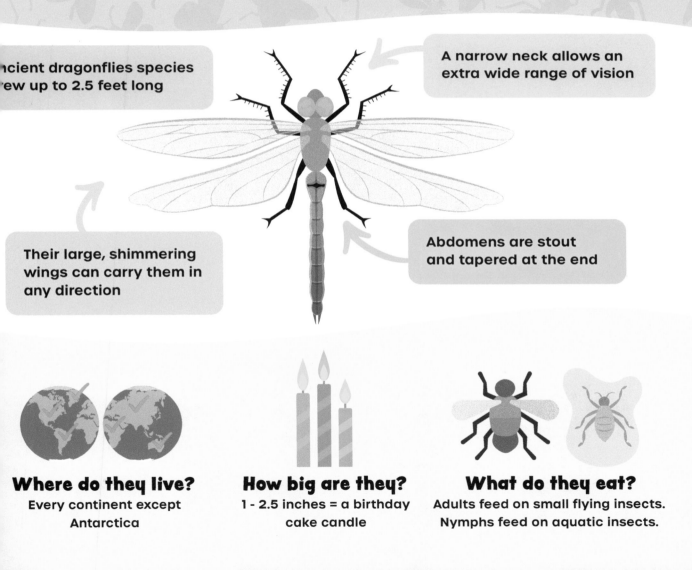

ncient dragonflies species rew up to 2.5 feet long

A narrow neck allows an extra wide range of vision

Their large, shimmering wings can carry them in any direction

Abdomens are stout and tapered at the end

## Where do they live?
Every continent except Antarctica

## How big are they?
1 - 2.5 inches = a birthday cake candle

## What do they eat?
Adults feed on small flying insects. Nymphs feed on aquatic insects.

# Firefly

*Lampyridae*

**Pictured is a Common Eastern Firefly (*Photinus pyralis*)**

# FUN FACTS

Fireflies produce light through a process called bio-luminescence. All larval forms of fireflies glow, but adults of some species do not glow. Different species produce different colors of light and flash patterns to communicate. Some species can even flash synchronously (at the same time)!

They have soft bodies that vary in size, shape, and color

Hard fore wings protect the hind wings which are used for flying

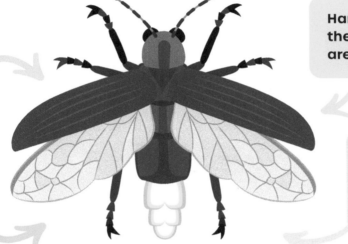

n many species, female fireflies are bigger than the males and do not have wings

Many species have a special organ that allows them to produce light

### Where do they live?
Every continent except Antarctica

### How big are they?
Up to 1 inch = a quarter

### What do they eat?
Adults feed on nectar and pollen, though some adults do not eat at all

# Jumping Spider

*Salticidae*

**Pictured is a Regal Jumping Spider (*Phidippus regius*)**

# FUN FACTS

Unlike some other species of spiders, jumping spiders do not build webs to catch prey. Instead, they ambush prey by jumping on them. Jumping spiders can jump a distance of 10-50 times their own body length!

They have 8 eyes total, with four particularly large ones in the front

They vary drastically in coloration from brown and black to showier shades of red, blue, and green

Some jumping spiders have mouth parts that are large and iridescent

The hair on their bodies help sense movement

**Where do they live?**
Every continent except Antarctica

**How big are they?**
Up to 1 inch = a postage stamp

**What do they eat?**
Insects and other spiders

# Swallowtail Butterfly

*Papilionidae*

**Pictured is a Eastern Tiger Swallowtail Butterfly (*Papilio glaucus*)**

# FUN FACTS

Swallowtail butterflies are among the largest butterflies in North America. Like all butterflies, swallowtails have a straw-like tongue called a proboscis which they use to sip nectar from flowers. When not in use, the proboscis coils up in a small spiral near the butterfly's head.

Swallowtail caterpillars are colored to mimic bird droppings as camouflage

Some species of swallowtails mimic the colors of poisonous butterflies for protection

Adults of some species feature "tails" on their hind wings

They come in a range of colors from black and yellow to iridescent blue

### Where do they live?
Every continent except Antarctica

### How big are they?
Wingspan up to 6 inches = a hot dog

### What do they eat?
Caterpillars (larvae) feed on host plants. Adults feed on nectar.

# Grasshopper

*Acrididae*

**Pictured is a American Grasshopper (*Schistocerca americana*)**

# FUN FACTS

Grasshoppers can make a chirping sound by rubbing their legs against their wings. Grasshoppers can hear the sounds of other grasshoppers using a simple eardrum called a tympanal organ, which is located on the grasshopper's abdomen.

he antennae
 their face
elp them
ouch, smell,
nd - in some
pecies - hear

Flying wings are folded neatly under leathery fore wings

They have medium to large slender and elongated bodies

Their strong hind legs help them jump up to 2.5 feet in the air

## Where do they live?
Every continent except Antarctica

## How big are they?
Up to 4 inches =
2 AA batteries

## What do they eat?
Plant leaves and flowers

# Mantidfly

*Mantispidae*

**Pictured is a Mantidfly (*Leptomantispa pulchella*)**

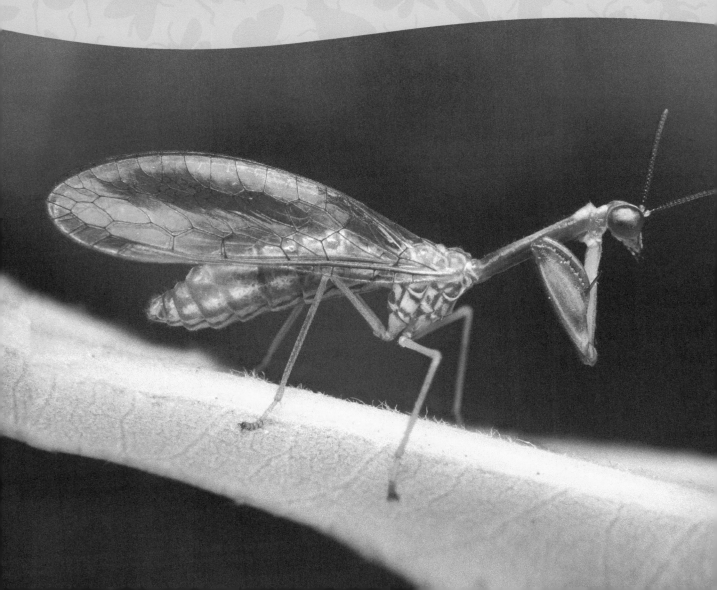

# FUN FACTS

Mantidflies get their name from their mantis-like appearance. Like praying mantises, mantidflies have claw-like, raptorial forelegs which they use to capture prey. Many species are nocturnal so you might find them near your porch lights at night.

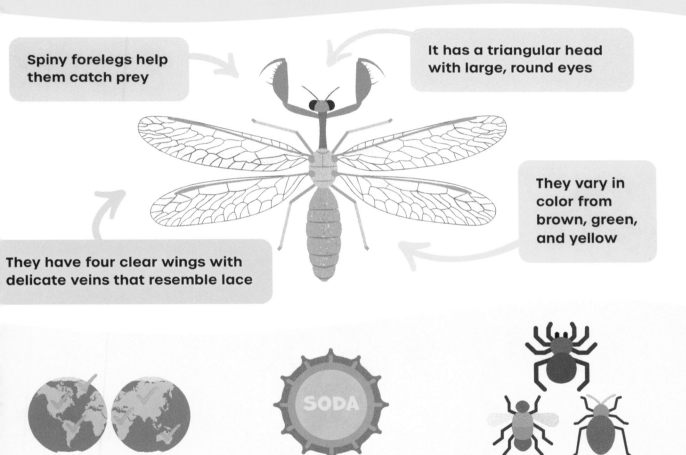

Spiny forelegs help them catch prey

It has a triangular head with large, round eyes

They vary in color from brown, green, and yellow

They have four clear wings with delicate veins that resemble lace

**Where do they live?**
Every continent except Antarctica

**How big are they?**
Up to 1 inch = a bottle cap

SODA

**What do they eat?**
Insects and spiders

# Skipper

*Hesperiidae*

**Pictured is a Peck's Skipper (*Polites peckius*)**

# FUN FACTS

Adult skippers are diurnal, skipping from plant to plant feeding on nectar during the day. Skipper caterpillars (larvae) feed under cover of night to avoid predation from birds.

...e way to ...entify them is ...y their short, ...ubbed antennae ...at end in small ...rves or hooks

Skippers are like a visual and behavioral blend between a butterfly and a moth

They vary in color from gray, white, brown, orange, and black

Their entire body is covered in hair

### Where do they live?
Every continent except Antarctica

### How big are they?
Wingspan up to 1.5 inches = a Lego mini-figure

### What do they eat?
Caterpillars (larvae) feed on host plants. Adults feed on nectar.

# Katydid

## *Tettigoniidae*

**Pictured is a Leaf Katydid (*Stilpnochlora* species)**

# FUN FACTS

Katydids are usually green and leaf-shaped, but some katydids appear yellow, orange, or even hot pink in coloration due to a genetic mutation. Katydids with this rare mutation have a hard time blending into their leafy surroundings.

When they rub their wings together they make a call that sounds like "ka-ty-did"

They have a body shape like a leaf, allowing them to blend into their environment

Antennae can be longer than the length of their body

Hind legs are much longer than their front legs to help them jump from plant to plant

### Where do they live?
Every continent except Antarctica

### How big are they?
Up to 2.5 inches = a house key

### What do they eat?
Most species eat plants but some feed on other insects

# Orb Weaver Spider

*Araneidae*

**Pictured is an Orb Weaver (*Araneus cingulatus*)**

# FUN FACTS

Orb weavers build spiral, wheel-shaped webs where they rest during the daytime. They are most active in the evening. Many species build a new web each day to ensure their webs are free of debris, allowing them to remain nearly invisible to prey.

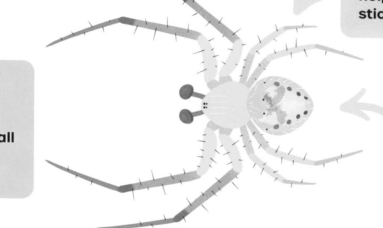

The hairs on its legs help prevent it from sticking to its own web

There are over 3,000 species of orb weaver spiders which all vary in shape, color, and size

Their large bodies can be reddish brown, green, gray, or golden in color

## Where do they live?
Every continent except Antarctica

## How big are they?
Average 1 inch body length = a quarter

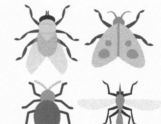

## What do they eat?
Small insects including flies, moths, beetles, and mosquitoes

# Paper Wasp

## *Vespidae*

**Pictured are Paper Wasps protecting their nest (*Polistes dorsalis*)**

# FUN FACTS

Like honey bees, paper wasps live in colonies. They build their papery nests by chewing dead wood or plant stems and mixing it with saliva. Nests often resemble umbrellas that have many cells for raising their young.

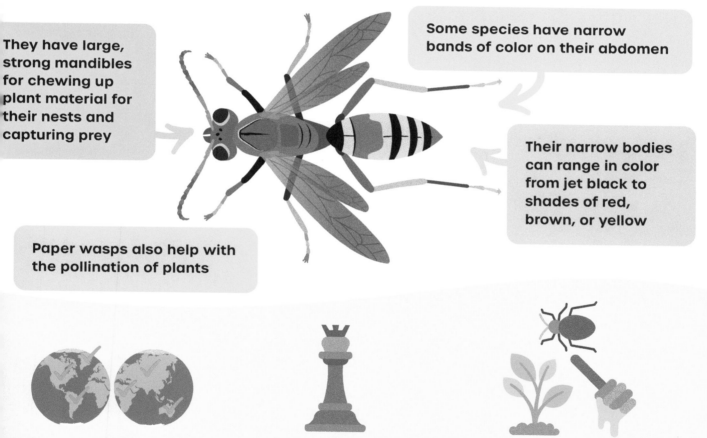

They have large, strong mandibles for chewing up plant material for their nests and capturing prey

Some species have narrow bands of color on their abdomen

Their narrow bodies can range in color from jet black to shades of red, brown, or yellow

Paper wasps also help with the pollination of plants

**Where do they live?**
Every continent except Antarctica

**How big are they?**
Up to 1.5 inches = a chess piece

**What do they eat?**

Nectar, pollen, and other insects

# Cicada

*Cicadidae*

**Pictured is a Periodical Cicada (*Magicicada* species)**

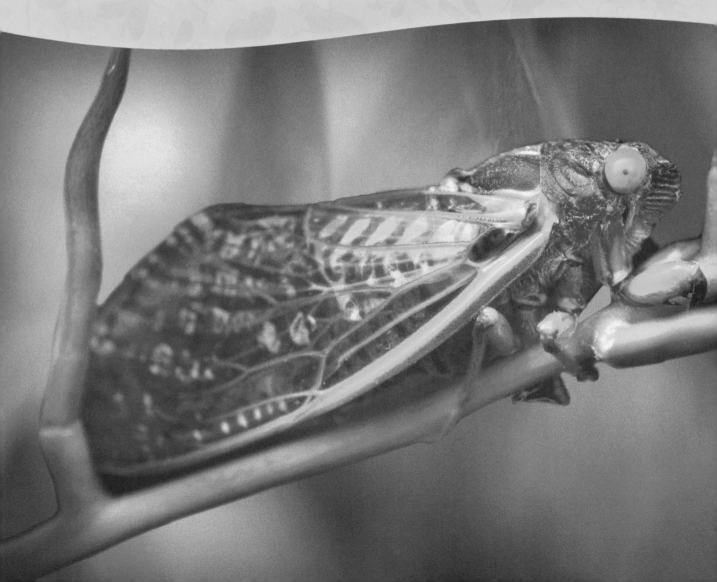

# FUN FACTS

Male cicadas create a mating call by expanding and contracting a special membrane on the abdomen called a tymbal. In some species, this mating call can reach over 100 decibels, which is as loud as a jackhammer!

They leave behind shells when they molt

Cicadas have the longest lifespan of any insect of 13-17 years

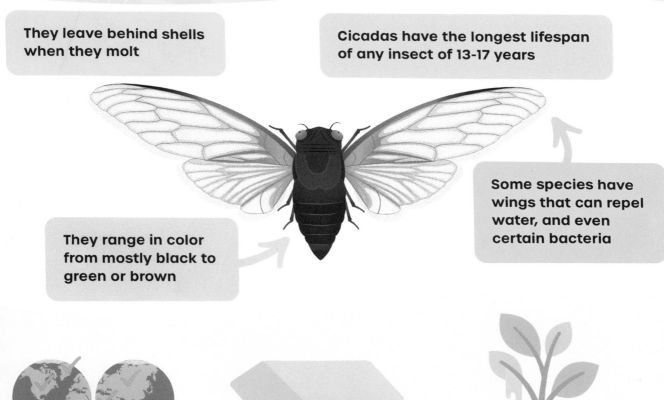

Some species have wings that can repel water, and even certain bacteria

They range in color from mostly black to green or brown

## Where do they live?
Every continent except Antarctica

## How big are they?
1-2 inches = an eraser

## What do they eat?
Plant sap